Library of Congress Number: 77-27109

1 2 3 4 5 6 7 8 9 0 82 81 80 79 78

Printed and bound in the United States of America.

Library of Congress Cataloging in Publication Data

Sawyer, Paul.
    There once was a book of limericks.

    SUMMARY: Presents twenty illustrated limericks and
instructions for writing these five-line verses.
    [1. Limericks — Juvenile literature. [1. Limericks]
I. Title.
PZ8.3.S248Th   811'.5'4   77-27109
ISBN 0-8172-1168-3 lib. bdg.

THERE ONCE WAS
A BOOK OF LIMERICKS

by Paul Sawyer

RAINTREE CHILDRENS BOOKS
Milwaukee · Toronto · Melbourne · London

INTRODUCTION

No one knows just when people began to write limericks. We don't even know how the limerick got its name. But we do know that people in England were writing limericks more than 150 years ago. The most famous collection of limericks, *A Book of Nonsense,* was written by Edward Lear in 1846.

You can recognize a limerick in several ways. For one thing, it usually is, or tries to be, funny. For another, it has a regular form. It always has five lines. The first, second and fifth lines rhyme. And the third and the fourth lines also rhyme. Usually the first, second and fifth lines have eight or nine syllables. The third and fourth lines have fewer syllables, usually five or six. (The word *dog* has one syllable. The word *monkey* has two syllables. The word *elephant* has three syllables.) Most of the limericks in this book have eight syllables in lines 1, 2, and 5, and five syllables in lines 3 and 4.

Why don't you try to write your own limericks? I'll show you how to do it. Let's suppose a boy tried his best to write a limerick but he couldn't do it. That will be the idea around which we'll build our limerick. What rhymes with *limerick? Dick.* So we'll begin with A *young boy by the name of Dick.* This line has eight syllables. Our second line could be *Tried to compose a limerick.* This also has eight syllables. Next, you can either write a fifth line, which must rhyme with *limerick* and *Dick,* or you can write the third and fourth lines. Let's do it the first

4

way. *Kick* rhymes with *Dick* and *limerick*. Since the boy couldn't finish the limerick, he would be angry with himself. We can write *He gave himself a good swift kick.* This line has eight syllables, just like lines one and two. Now we turn our attention to lines three and four. Remember that they must rhyme and have either five or six syllables. How about *Since he spent so much time / Without finding a rhyme*? The two lines rhyme and each one has six syllables. The limerick is complete:

> A young boy by the name of Dick
> Tried to compose a limerick.
> Since he spent so much time
> Without finding a rhyme
> He gave himself a good swift kick.

Not great, but it's all right for a starter. Let's see whether you can do better.

Have fun reading the limericks in this book and trying to write some of your own.

There once lived Alfred, a lion,
Who told his friends he was dyin'.
He sank to the ground,
And looked all around.
They found he really was lyin'.

A cute little girl named Jenny
Loved money but didn't have any.
Mom told her, "You may
Do some chores each day,
And so earn many a penny."

There was a cute monkey named Mast,
Who was so remarkably fast.
One day he grew sick
And being so quick
In less than a day he passed.

You know about litter, for sure.
It's a disease without a cure.
But maybe some day
We'll find a good way,
In books about litter-a-ture.

13

Tom, a very bad-tempered child,
Never had any moments mild.
Teachers he saddened,
Friends he maddened,
And worse, he drove his parents wild.

14

A horse by the name of Ranto
Galloping began to panto.
I said, "Please embrace
An easier pace."
"So sorry," he said, "I canto."

A young girl by the name of Marr
Thought she'd like to visit a star.
Her two arms she beat
And kicked hard her feet,
But soon found she didn't get far.

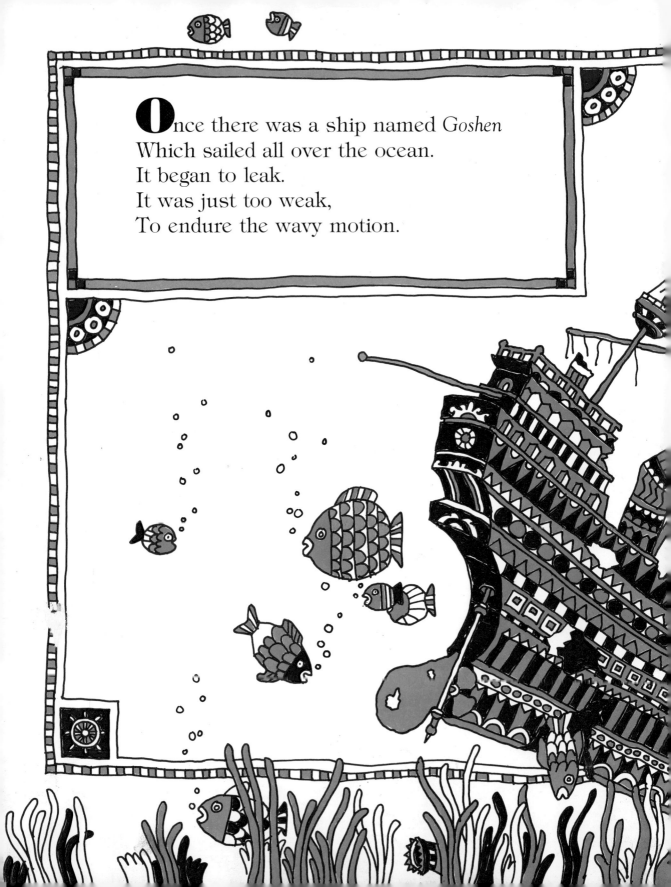

Once there was a ship named *Goshen*
Which sailed all over the ocean.
It began to leak.
It was just too weak,
To endure the wavy motion.

One day Bill bought himself a steak
Which his wife was supposed to bake.
The flame was too high.
Smoke reached to the sky.
Poor Bill had to eat her mistake.

Ken had an ache in his tummy,
So he ran to tell his mummy.
"You know what you did?
You poor little kid.
You ate the dog's food, you dummy."

25

There was once a rabbit named Guy,
Unable to swim or to fly.
He couldn't think straight,
Yet strange to relate,
He was able to multiply.

There were six birds perched on a fence.
Now let's see if you're bright or dense.
Two birds flew away.
The rest chose to stay.
Two or four left — which makes more sense?

29

A talkative young boy named Lum
Once upon a time was struck dumb.
No reason at all,
As I can recall.
It's just that the words would not come.

A gigantic young boy named Lear
Was embarrassed one day to hear
His close friends say, "You
Will need one more shoe.
You've grown another foot this year."

Two little trains named Huff and Puff
Used to carry all kinds of stuff.
"To pull we are hired.
But we feel so tired,"
They grumbled. "Enough is enough."

My cat and my dog like to fight.
To see them is really a sight.
The cat will just sit,
Then he'll hiss and spit,
And suddenly the dog takes flight.

The best thing for anyone's nose
Is to take a sniff of a rose.
I'm sure you'll agree
With adults like me
It smells a lot better than toes.

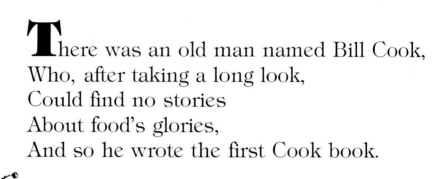

There was an old man named Bill Cook,
Who, after taking a long look,
Could find no stories
About food's glories,
And so he wrote the first Cook book.

41

42

One day I was wearing a sweater.
The weather was getting no better.
To say it quite plain,
It began to rain,
And I became wetter and wetter.

There once was a terrible crime.
A foolish old man murdered time.
He stomped on a clock
And then threw a rock.
Alas! Now I'm stumped for a rhyme.

Photography Credits